A Light ˙

MW01243792

Back cover picture credit: Morgan Phillips

ISBN: 9798639291791

Peacemaking - Peacekeeping

A Light Theology About Human Conflict

Forward

This book came out of a sermon series I did for the church I pastor. My church is no different than other churches I imagine. The church I pastor is filled with red-blooded people who work hard at relationships, and some times fail at relationships. During a particularly busy season of counseling I felt it necessary to deal as a church with some basics when it comes to resolving conflicts with others. As we wrapped up the series, many of our congregants asked if they could have my notes. We responded to this request with this book. Most of the concepts in this book were born in conversations with my dear wife, Annie. Together, we have spent countless hours trying to help families, couples and friends learn how to communicate and resolve differences. Indeed, Annie and I have spent countless hours working through our own differences. She truly is my partner in ministry, and the love of my life. I dedicate this book to her. Annie and I truly hope the concepts in this book will be a blessing to you and the relationships in your life. As I will state in the conclusion, relationships are a long term investment. We hope and pray that you will commit to the long term plan of loving, rebuilding and restoring.

Blessings,

Pastor Rob

Peacemaking - Peacekeeping

A Light Theology About Human Conflict

Introduction

I always have anxiety issues when I walk into a hardware store. It is not because I don't know what I'm looking for (although I generally don't). I usually feel anxious because I am dressed in office attire and not construction attire. This usually means I will receive some unnecessary and unsolicited explaining (some call this "mansplaining") and the look of annoyance along with the rolling eyes. On one particular day however, I was able to experience the awkwardness of watching someone else have to deal with shaming. I happened to be in the lumber aisle that day as I was looking for some pressure treated boards to use on the deck I was repairing. There was a man inspecting boards in the same aisle as me, taking each board out and checking its quality to see if it had a natural bow or if it was straight. He obviously knew what he was doing but was not dressed the part so when a worker at the store arrived to try to help him he was obviously annoyed. What happened next would serve as a text book case study in human conflicts. The boards he was inspecting were in the wrong section. They were high quality boards that should have been in another section, but had been placed in the section with the lower quality and less expensive boards. The attendant noticed this problem and proceeded to remind the customer that he would not receive the price he was hoping for. They both started saying more, and listening less. They both started talking more loudly and with a higher pitch. By the time it was done, the customer was having a temper tantrum that would make a 4 year old jealous. He was stamping his foot and yelling "I want what I want, and I want it now"! This is not an exaggeration and those were his exact words. My 5 year old and one of my teenage daughters were with me and began to laugh. I quickly ushered them out of the aisle for safety reasons.

Human conflict can arise so quickly and without warning that we are not prepared for the mayhem. Human conflict can also brim slowly to the surface over years and years of unspoken annoyance.

As a pastor, I have counseled with quite a few married couples who suddenly find themselves in a broken relationship because one of the spouses has suddenly had enough of something he or she has been bothered by for months or years. When they finally get honest, their hearts have already set like flint and they are moving on from the relationship because of the emotional affair of the better life they think they need.

The reality is that most of the counseling I do in my office and in homes has to do with human conflicts. I am not just talking about marriage conflicts. I have counseled through business conflicts, parent and child

A Light Theology About Human Conflict

conflicts, conflicts between neighbors and of course many, many church conflicts. Anywhere you find two humans living in close proximity to one another you will find two humans that will eventually have to work through a conflict. Social media has compounded the issue, as we can end up in an argument with someone we have never met who lives a continent away!

The biggest problem with human conflict is that we are not taught how to work through it. We certainly do not see productive conflict resolution modeled for us. Television rarely emulates restored relationships and usually glorifies self gratification to the point that it elevates adultery and divorce. Reality TV instigates fights and broken relationships. Politicians model arrogance, argument and slander. Athletes trash-talk and fight. Video games promote violence.

When you read the Bible you begin to see in the book of Acts a church that wanted to be different from the violent culture it was immersed in. While people slaughtered one another in the colosseum and politicians betrayed and murdered one another, the early church began to be seen as "those of a different way" (Acts 18:26; 24:14). The early church certainly had conflict, which is why every epistle written to the early church deals in some way with people in conflict; but every epistle also gave the root reason why it was so important for believers to work at living together in

Peacemaking - Peacekeeping

harmony and working to restore broken relationships. The reason in one word was: Gospel. The Gospel presented the good news that God had sent his only Son into the world to restore our broken relationship with him. God wants us to have the same kind of relationship with him that Adam and Eve enjoyed with him in the Garden of Eden. To solve the conflicted relationship we have with Him because of sin, God sent Jesus to die in our place on the cross. Jesus entered the conflict we started and died because of that conflict.

Paul instructed the church at Philippi (in his letter called Philippians) to live with one another in the same sacrifice and humility that Jesus modeled for us while on this earth. This pursuit of sacrificial love and grace brought the early church together in a way that the entire world began to notice. God has called us to the same type of pursuit today.

My goal in this book two-fold: to help the reader understand how they ought to approach human conflicts in their life, and also to understand that human conflict is both necessary and useful in becoming more like Jesus in our lives. Not all relationships can be restored on earth, but it is important that we understand our role and responsibility in every conflict. I hope and pray that this book will be a blessing to you and a tool for you to

A Light Theology About Human Conflict

use as you seek to honor God by living in harmony with others.

Chapter 1 - Why Human Conflict is Important and Necessary

I sat there in the pizza shop with my 7 year old son and 5 teenage boys from our church youth group. We had just enjoyed a church work day and I wanted to say "thank you" to the boys for a job well done, so lunch was the reward of choice. As we waited for the food to arrive the boys began to look for a way to expend their testosterone-rich nervous energy. They proceeded to do what so many boys their age have done since the beginning of time, they engaged in aggressive and physical behaviors to prove their male bravado. Bloody knuckles was the game of choice, followed by a game called "slaps". I sat in the precarious position of letting it go long enough for all to realize this was dumb and stepping in before permanent damage could be done. Lesson learned? I think not. At the end of it all the boys were laughing, comparing battle wounds and strangely enough, more tight knit than they were 15 minutes earlier. What I had just witnessed was human conflict bringing young men together. That is, after all, the nature of sport.

In a very real way, human conflict by nature brings humanity together. There would be no conflict if humans lived completely autonomously from each other in solitary confinement. We must understand that human conflict can have the power to either divide humanity, or unite humanity.

Conflict brings division, but it can also bring connection!

Much of the New Testament is written to address human conflict. If you have ever attended a church faithfully, then you have probably witnessed people problems because people have problems and churches are filled with people. This has always been the case since the founding of the church in the time of the book of Acts. I don't believe that Human conflict is just a flawed outcome of sin. I sincerely believe conflict is part of the design of God's work of redemption with humanity and vital to a believer's sanctification in Christ. Over the next few chapters I would like to look at some of the Apostles' teachings on conflict, starting with the book of Romans. As we get started, I want to point out 4 reasons why human conflicts are necessary to our connected spiritual lives from Romans 12.

Peacemaking - Peacekeeping

4 Reasons Human Conflicts are Necessary

Romans 12:1-2 (ESV)

I appeal to you therefore, brothers, by the mercies of God, to present your bodies as a living sacrifice, holy and acceptable to God, which is your spiritual worship. 2 Do not be conformed to this world, but be transformed by the renewal of your mind, that by testing you may discern what is the will of God, what is good and acceptable and perfect.

1. Human conflict follows the path of Christ. (vs 1)

When you retrace the steps of the Savior, it is plain to see that from the moment he arrived to the moment of his death, there was conflict surrounding him at every moment. Herod the king tried to have him killed. His own people in Nazareth tried to have him thrown off of a cliff. The religious leaders continually sought to destroy him and eventually had him executed with the help of the Romans.

A Light Theology About Human Conflict

The Scriptures give consistent instruction to walk in the path of Christ, seeking to live the life he lived. (Phil. 2, I Peter 2) Ultimately, the chief defining characteristic of Jesus Christ's life on earth was willing sacrifice.

Paul calls us here in Romans 12:1 to follow in the pattern of Jesus as a "living sacrifice" and he calls this a "mercy" of God that results in worship.

Paul calls it a mercy because he views it as a privilege that results in worship.

The Old Testament sacrificial system was more than just obedience and repentance, it was also worship. The altar of incense signified prayer and worship going up to God, a worship that took place as the people brought their sin offerings and lambs of atonement. Jesus was the ultimate fulfillment of the sacrificial system as the Passover Lamb, bringing both payment of sin and atonement for believers as well as great glory to God. When we follow in Christ's footsteps as a living sacrifice, *we* bring glory to God as well. This is why Paul calls it a worship!

Paul calls it a worship because it reflects the character of God through Jesus.

How does this involve human conflict and what is the connection to Romans 12:1-2?   Living in Human harmony through grace and love is the entire context of the rest of the chapter as Paul writes about the marks of a true Christian.

2. Human conflict keeps us honest with our purpose for living. (vs 2a)

Paul begins this verse with a juxtaposition - Don't be conformed, rather be transformed. The word "conformed" is the greek word syschēmatizō. It is a compound word that means "to fashion yourself like the group".

If you grew up in the 1980's like me, you will understand this concept well. We wore our stone washed jeans in such a way that our pant legs were tight-rolled. This meant you had to flip the front of your jeans over to the side, and then role from the bottom keeping the appearance of a very sleek leg line. In the early 1990's I moved from Los Angeles, California to backwoods central Florida. We had stopped rolling our jeans (or stone washing them for that matter) around 1988 in Los Angeles. In 1992, when I walked into my sophomore year of high school at a new school in Florida., I had regular legged pants on, but everyone thought I had bell bottom jeans on because they weren't tight rolled. I had to go back in time almost 5 years to "fit in" or be conformed to the social group.

A Light Theology About Human Conflict

This is a great illustration of conformity to the world. In a reverse way, living as a believer can seem very much like going back in time. The way we act and react, live and love can seem antiquated or even foreign, and often to keep up appearances we are pressured to conform to the world's standard of living.

The word "transformed" is the greek word metamorphoō. It is another compound greek word that means to form something new after a time, and it is the exact description of the process of a butterfly coming out of its chrysalis. When we as believers receive Christ and identify with him, we are formed into something new and different and out of the old. (see Gal. 5 and Romans 13). Paul is forcing the issue here of being identified with something new and different from the rest of the world. This harkens back to the early church being called the "Hodos" or "those of a different way" (Acts 19:23). Paul speaks throughout Ephesians of walking in a different way, the way of Christ and love.

We are called to live life in a transformed way from the worldly pattern, and human conflict allows that opportunity. It forces that opportunity!

Human conflict forces us to either react selfishly and with anger, or to walk the way of love and grace in the manner of Jesus Christ. This is the honest way that reflects our new natures.

3. Human conflict forces us to prioritize God's will. (vs 2b)

Paul uses the word "testing" here. The word "test" is the greek word dokimazō. This was the word used for the process of examining money or legal documents to be sure they were genuine. ("Documentation" comes from this Greek concept.) The grocery store clerk does this today with the $100 bills and the brown marking pen.

Human conflict allows you to see if you are genuine in your faith. It is a necessary test of how much you are willing to trust God.

It causes us to ask ourselves if we trust that God is big enough to break down walls and build bridges, or if we love God enough to afford him the opportunity. Ultimately when we don't trust God or love him more than our comfort, we choose to either fight angrily on in conflict or run away from conflict.

4. Human conflict forces us to depend on God and His Word for wisdom. (vs 2c)

We cannot know what is good and acceptable and perfect in our actions and reactions without looking to God and His Word, and human conflict forces us to have to ask for wisdom! The book of Proverbs was given as a wisdom book for dealing with human conflict!

A Light Theology About Human Conflict

Solomon was known as a king with great wisdom, so he wrote the book of Proverbs to help his sons (future rulers of Israel) know how to conduct themselves in a way befitting the responsibility of the throne. Much of what Solomon gave by way of wisdom was about dealing with human conflict.

It is important to understand that if you were going to put wisdom into an equation, it would look something like this:

Wisdom = Knowledge + Experience

Solomon knew that his sons would need knowledge of how to deal with difficult people and issues, but that knowledge would not be enough. Solomon knew that his sons would also need the experience they did not yet have to apply this knowledge properly. When we ask for wisdom, we are asking either for knowledge we don't yet possess, or experience we have not yet earned, or both.

Peacemaking - Peacekeeping

Proverbs 3:1-6 teaches that the wisdom of God is a better support system and guide for the human condition than our own worldly wisdom!

Proverbs 3:1-6 (ESV)

My son, do not forget my teaching,

but let your heart keep my commandments,

2 for length of days and years of life

and peace they will add to you.

3 Let not steadfast love and faithfulness forsake you;

bind them around your neck;

write them on the tablet of your heart.

4 So you will find favor and good success

in the sight of God and man.

5 Trust in the LORD with all your heart,

and do not lean on your own understanding.

6 In all your ways acknowledge him,

and he will make straight your paths.

The key to this passage is found in verses 5 and 6. If we don't trust the Lord for wisdom, then we will rely on our own perceived wisdom rooted in worldly advice.

A Light Theology About Human Conflict

There might be some helpful information found there, but ultimately it will fall short of the way and walk of the Savior. Sooner or later, the world's advice always leads to selfish ambition or anger.

This will require both honesty and humility, just as a weak and broken person using a cane to walk, or someone needing directions (vs 6).

I suffer from osteoarthritis throughout my entire body. God, in his sovereign design has currently chosen for me to dwell in upstate New York as I write this book. The winters here can be brutal, and they aggravate my arthritis in such a way that I am reduced to walking with a cane during the peak winter months. It is both humiliating and frustrating, but every time I abandon the cane during these conditions I inevitably fall or make my issues worse. In these moments I have to accept that I need the crutch, I need help, until my body has recovered or the weather has changed.

As a male, I believe the greatest invention of our time has been GPS. In our extensive traveling in ministry over the years, I have found it humiliating and annoying to stop and ask for directions. GPS has afforded me the privilege of self sufficient pride in finding my away around.

In conflict, there are many times when we must humble ourselves and seek the crutch and guide of God's

Peacemaking - Peacekeeping

wisdom from his Word and his people. Human conflict forces this reckoning upon us, and it is a grace of God!

James, the faithful pastor of the very difficult Jerusalem church put it this way:

James 1:2-8 (ESV)

2 Count it all joy, my brothers, when you meet trials of various kinds, 3 for you know that the testing of your faith produces steadfastness. 4 And let steadfastness have its full effect, that you may be perfect and complete, lacking in nothing. 5 If any of you lacks wisdom, let him ask God, who gives generously to all without reproach, and it will be given him. 6 But let him ask in faith, with no doubting, for the one who doubts is like a wave of the sea that is driven and tossed by the wind. 7 For that person must not suppose that he will receive anything from the

A Light Theology About Human Conflict

> Lord; [8] he is a double-
> minded man, unstable in all
> his ways.

I hope that if you have found this book you not only have reached for it because you are in conflict (it is a gift), but that you are also reaching out for wisdom and hope in your conflict from The One who wants to redeem all circumstances for his glory. Take a moment to prepare your heart in prayer. I would encourage you not to read any further until you have meditated on these words and asked God to make them sincere in your heart.

Prayer of Application: "God, give me the honesty and humility I need to seek for your wisdom in dealing with my human conflicts."

Chapter 2 - How Human Conflict Defines Roles and Boundaries

You stay in your social box, and I'll stay in mine....

I'm the kind of guy who needs space, especially in social settings. When someone comes up to me and puts their face close to mine, I wince and step backwards. Add two hands on my shoulders and I am liable to respond with a ninja move propelling you backwards and onwards. I'm a social introvert, so it is already a big ask for me to be moderately social for long periods of time. I can sustain some unnecessary chatter, but I need my space. Grant me the safety of my spacial box and I will give you at least enough time to nod my head and make every effort to be interested in words.

All joking aside, if autonomy brings no connection and therefore no conflict, then the opposite is true that conflict arises from not understanding boundaries and roles.

There are many of us, if not most of us who can appreciate certain boundaries. I love food trays that separate my food. I love when my apple sauce does not run into my mashed potatoes. I love what I would call "armrest-bordering" on airplanes and in movie theaters. I once researched armrest etiquette while

A Light Theology About Human Conflict

sitting next to someone who was taking my armrest. They had the audacity to take the window seat on our plane and both armrests. I was in the middle seat and felt I deserved the right to both of my armrests. I showed restraint for the Gospel's sake.

I grew up in a home with three boys. This is a recipe for conflict disaster, especially when your dad is a traveling evangelist who keeps his sons trapped in a back seat of a station wagon for 8 hours at a time before personal entertainment devices have been invented. When you are sitting in a bench seat with two brothers, there are certain rules of decorum. Rule 1: Thou shalt not cross the imaginary line into thine brothers personal space. Rule 2: The middle seat shall receive, by default, more personal space than the window seats. Rule 3: If thine brother encroaches on thine personal space, thou shalt have the right, nay, the responsibility to put thine brother in his place with a swift slap to the face. Rule 4: If a fight doth ensue, the paternal pilot (dad) is obligated to wave his arm furiously behind him and across all passengers in the bench seat until said fight has ceased.

There are important reasons to establish boundaries, especially in the cases of abuse or dishonesty in relationships. Roles are also important as they help us understand both responsibilities and accountability within human social constructs. We need to understand both *boundaries* and *roles* within every human setting. That being said, dealing with human conflict has just as much to do with understating our own box as it does keeping our neighbors in theirs. In this chapter we will seek to understand why accepting the boundaries and roles of both ourselves and others has to do with understanding our identity in Christ.

If we are going to work through conflicts, we must understand our identity in Christ.

In chapter one I sought to help us understand that <u>conflict brings division, but it can also bring connection!</u> Human conflict can bring connection because it is intended to bring restoration. The conflict of the cross brought restoration to the garden relationship God originally created and fostered with mankind. That original relationship which was so free and wonderful was built on an understanding of roles and boundaries. The role of Adam and Eve was to worship God though receiving and depending on his gift of the garden relationship. Their boundary was to honor God by not taking of the forbidden fruit of pride and selfishness. The original boundary was not to keep them confined in the garden, but rather to keep them away from one single tree. Just as we do today, they reversed the boundaries in their own minds through the deception of the snake, and believed that God was keeping them from everything, when in reality he was keeping them from only one thing. That one thing ultimately cursed the entire human race due to Adam's disobedience.

In chapter two I want to help us understand how human conflicts can help define roles and boundaries.

How human conflicts can help define roles and boundaries.

Preface: when I mention roles and boundaries, I'm not speaking about others; I am speaking about you and me! We need to understand our roles and boundaries with regards to the love and leading of the Holy Spirit. What is a role? A role is a part in society that you play: husband, wife, parent, child, sister, brother, boss, employee, citizen, neighbor and the list goes on and on. All of these titles have a part, or role, to play within the human social construct. Any of these roles can be manipulated and extended beyond their rightful reach, or boundary. Our boundaries are determined by the rights and responsibilities within these roles. Conflict arises when either pride or selfishness tell me to act in a way that either takes on more than my role has been defined as, or I ignore and/or push back against the rightful role of another.

I spoke in the last chapter about living in a different way than the rest of the world. Paul called it being

Peacemaking - Peacekeeping

transformed instead of conformed. The biggest way we do this is through humility.

It must be stated that you will never learn to resolve human conflicts in your life until you resolve to learn the humility of Christ!

To grasp this concept, we now look to the next section of verses in Romans 12.

Romans 12:3-8 (ESV)

3 For by the grace given to me I say to everyone among you not to think of himself more highly than he ought to think, but to think with sober judgment, each according to the measure of faith that God has assigned. 4 For as in one body we have many members, and the members do not all have the same function, 5 so we, though many, are one body in Christ, and individually members one of another. 6 Having gifts that differ according to the grace given to us, let us use them:

A Light Theology About Human Conflict

> if prophecy, in proportion to
> our faith; 7 if service, in our
> serving; the one who
> teaches, in his teaching;
> 8 the one who exhorts, in his
> exhortation; the one who
> contributes, in generosity;
> the one who leads, with
> zeal; the one who does acts
> of mercy, with cheerfulness.

Paul began his thought on roles within the church with the need for humility! (vs 3)

Paul used a descriptive phrase to describe humility: sober judgment! In the greek language it reads "thinking *into and through* sobriety", as opposed to "thinking *out of* sobriety". Paul understood that we naturally self inflate. It is more natural to see ourselves as better and bigger rather than lesser and leaner. We naturally speak out of the drunkenness of self inflation and expectation rather than the sober reality of who we really are. Paul reminds us here that we need to work towards a more humble view of ourselves! We need to practice humility when we act and react.

Out of humility Paul then used an illustration of what people living together in humility looks like: a body performing in proper health! (vs 4-5) Paul gave a similar teaching in 1 Corinthians 12 where he talked about all the parts of one body being important, even though some parts are parts we can not see and do not give much attention to. He spoke almost humorously of the idea of the eye going on strike because it does not get to be a hand, and the nose going on strike because it does not get to be an ear. Paul understood that harmony in a group requires humility, and humility requires a sober view of our own self worth. A sober view of our own self worth requires a proper understanding of the Gospel. The Gospel teaches me to find my identity in the value of Christ and not myself.

Just as you will never resolve conflicts without a resolve for humility, you will never have humility until your identity is wrapped up in the identity of Christ.

To find my identity in Christ, I must see myself as God sees me. If I have asked Jesus to be my Savior, then my identity should be wrapped up in the reality that Christ's righteousness rests upon me. This means that God sees me with the same identity that he sees his own son, Jesus. God sees me as pure and spotless. 2 Corinthians 5:21(ESV) states "[21] For our sake he made him to be sin who knew no sin, so that in him we might become the righteousness of God." This means that our identity of sin has been traded for Christ's identity of righteousness. I must now remember that identity in

A Light Theology About Human Conflict

spite of how I may view myself, or even how others may view me. What God sees in me is more important that how I am seen on this earth. How God sees me informs how I should live on this earth. I should live with the identity of Christ in view. Every decision, every response or reaction, every act towards other people should reflect the identity of Christ upon me.

Paul closes his teaching on humility by stating that we should learn to appreciate how God has designed or "gifted" us and be settled in that identity, or role. (vs 6-8) Some of the most conflicted people I meet are people who can not accept their lives as God has designed them. They always want to be someone else or live someone else's life. This is more than just a teaching on self awareness, this is also a teaching on others awareness! If I can understand and appreciate my role, then I can also learn to understand and appreciate your role.

Human conflict always begins when one or more people misunderstand or disregard roles and boundaries.

The first step in working through conflict is humbly asking ourselves if we are the source of the conflict. **We must ask ourselves "Am I the one exceeding my boundaries and role in this relationship?"** It may be that you have crossed boundaries and taken liberties.

Peacemaking - Peacekeeping

It does not mean that the person you are in conflict with is innocent, but you can not deal with their issues unless you are ready to deal with your own. Jesus taught this in his teaching of the mote and speck parable in Matthew 7.

The second step in working through conflict is to honestly assess if there really is a conflict. **We must ask ourselves "Has the other person truly exceeded their own role and/or boundaries?"** It is important to note that you may not like the role and boundaries of the person you are in conflict with, but that does not mean they are wrong. This can be a difficult situation to accept! If you are not ready to humbly admit your own discovered faults then you are not interested in conflict resolution, you are interested in winning at all costs.

I have both experienced and witnessed neighborly disputes where one neighbor cries foul with the boundary lines, and after calling for a survey ends up finding out they had even less property than they currently thought they had. It is an important analogy of life: do not seek to move fences until you first understand why they are there.

A Light Theology About Human Conflict

Wisdom from Proverbs:

Proverbs 3:7 (ESV)

"Be not wise in your own eyes; fear the LORD, and turn away from evil."

Unless we let go of our drunken self view, we cannot honor the Lord and depart from evil! Where there is no resolve for humility, there is no resolving conflict!

Proverbs 3:34 (ESV)

"Toward the scorners he is scornful, but to the humble he gives favor."

To scorn means to arrogantly mock or deride. God brings scorn to those who hold on to their pride, but he brings favor in conflict to those who exercise humility.

Conflict can end in absolute disgrace. In worldly wisdom we tend to escalate conflict, but with God's humble wisdom we are able to dial down the rhetoric and work towards peaceful resolution. Look at the following proverbs that promote humble wisdom.

Proverbs 11:2 (ESV)

"When pride comes, then comes disgrace, but with the humble is wisdom."

Peacemaking - Peacekeeping

Proverbs 15:33 (ESV)

"The fear of the LORD is instruction in wisdom, and humility comes before honor."

Proverbs 18:12 (ESV)

"Before destruction a man's heart is haughty, but humility comes before honor."

Proverbs 27:2 (ESV)

"Let another praise you, and not your own mouth; a stranger, and not your own lips."

Proverbs 22:4 (ESV)

"The reward for humility and fear of the LORD is riches and honor and life."

Remember, these are truth sayings, not prophesies. We are not guaranteed wealth through humility. If that were the case, we would all be humble for selfish reasons, which is not humility!

The book of Proverbs has some important things to say about seeking advice in conflict. Look at this verse:

Proverbs 12:15 (ESV)

"The way of a fool is right in his own eyes, but a wise man listens to advice."

A Light Theology About Human Conflict

Some of the most foolish people I have counseled are people who come into my office for wisdom and then tune out everything except the voice inside their own minds. The Bible says this is foolish. We need wisdom outside our own minds if we are going to navigate conflicts.

As we have already seen, the test of conflict is both important and necessary to reveal what God is doing and needs to do in our hearts and lives. To respond well, it requires both humility and an acknowledgement that we need to be neither more nor less than who God has created us to be. We must ask ourselves what the boundaries and roles of our lives really are, and seek to honor God within those fences until he expands our roles and boarders. He will defend our rights. He will exalt our status should he choose to do so.

Is there ever a cause to do battle for the justice of boundaries and roles? There certainly are circumstances like these. In future chapters we will discuss what those circumstances are.

Let us close this chapter with a scripture and prayer. Once again, glean from Pastor James in his admonishment to the Jerusalem church.

Peacemaking - Peacekeeping

James 1:2-8 (ESV)

9 Let the lowly brother boast
in his exaltation, 10 and the
rich in his humiliation,
because like a flower of the
grass he will pass away.
11 For the sun rises with its
scorching heat and withers
the grass; its flower falls,
and its beauty perishes. So
also will the rich man fade
away in the midst of his
pursuits. 12 Blessed is the
man who remains steadfast
under trial, for when he has
stood the test he will
receive the crown of life,
which God has promised to
those who love him. 13 Let
no one say when he is
tempted, "I am being
tempted by God," for God
cannot be tempted with evil,
and he himself tempts no
one. 14 But each person is
tempted when he is lured
and enticed by his own
desire. 15 Then desire when

it has conceived gives birth to sin, and sin when it is fully grown brings forth death. [16] Do not be deceived, my beloved brothers. [17] Every good gift and every perfect gift is from above, coming down from the Father of lights, with whom there is no variation or shadow due to change. [18] Of his own will he brought us forth by the word of truth, that we should be a kind of firstfruits of his creatures.

Prayer of Application: "Lord, give me the humility I need to remove the specks of sin in my own eyes before I seek to correct the vision of my brothers and sisters. Give me the wisdom to understand my own role and boundaries, that I may not move the fences you have placed around me."

Chapter 3 - How Human Conflict Defines Love

When I was a kid my grandfather used to take me and my two brothers to the circus. There is a lot going on at a circus, probably more than a kid my age could take in and understand. One thing I did understand is that the clowns could not be trusted.

A lot of people are scared of clowns. This reality should not surprise us when one considers the psychological complexities of a smiling-faced human beating and lighting on fire another smiling faced human. I could not get over the exaggerated smiles mingled with the scary violence. Perhaps this is why we are fascinated with the Joker character in the Batman comics.

I think much of our human conflicts could be characterized in this way. Two or more people pretending to be happy and kind while they secretly bash one another in back rooms and church lobbies. By the time the confrontation happens, you have two people lighting one another on fire with big smiles trying to plead their own innocence.

A British band called the Platters first recorded a song that Freddy Mercury later made famous. The lyrics capture the mistrust we all struggle with as it refers to

A Light Theology About Human Conflict

humans as clowns, or the great pretenders that we all tend to be.

All too often we pretend everything is fine in public social settings while a world of angst festers in our hearts. When we finally let the poison out, it is too much to deal with so we say and do things we will probably regret.

In chapter one I began with the theological understanding that conflict brings division, but it can also bring connection because conflict is intended to bring restoration. The conflict of the cross brought restoration to the garden relationship God originally created and fostered with mankind!

In chapter 2 I pointed out that human conflicts can help define roles and boundaries. Remember, you will never learn to resolve human conflicts in your life until you resolve to learn the humility of Christ and your identity in Christ.

In this chapter I want to look at the truth that **Human Conflict Defines True Love.**

Let's start by looking at the next few verses in Romans 12.

Peacemaking - Peacekeeping

Romans 12:9-13 (ESV)

9 Let love be genuine.
Abhor what is evil; hold fast
to what is good. 10 Love one
another with brotherly
affection. Outdo one
another in showing honor.
11 Do not be slothful in zeal,
be fervent in spirit, serve the
Lord. 12 Rejoice in hope, be
patient in tribulation, be
constant in prayer.
13 Contribute to the needs of
the saints and seek to show
hospitality.

Paul now shifts to the practical side of dealing with human relationships. Everything else in this chapter is tangible and practical. Paul Starts off by telling the church to practice genuine love. The word "genuine" is the word anypokritos (ä-nü-po'-krē-tos) and the best description of this word I have seen is "not an act" or "not play acting". Love that flows from a human effort is not sustainable. We can pretend to love people through tolerance, but eventually the love of self will override any attempt at love for others and we will begin to lose our patience. Genuine love can only flow from one source. The apostle John said it this way in

A Light Theology About Human Conflict

his first epistle: "We love because He first loved us!" (I John 4:19) Human conflicts allow us to see and understand the true source of our love. If I am going to resolve conflict, or live in less conflict, I must first seek to love God before I can love people. Allow me to illustrate this concept with a diagram:

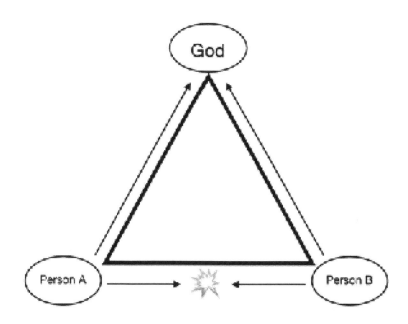

When we look at a person we are in conflict with, and try to adjust their behaviors to benefit our ability to love them, the result is often catastrophic. Why should you expect that they will respect your assessments of their behavior? We all tend to think we are the ones in the right. We all tend to think we have the moral, philosophical or theological high ground. Conversely, when two people both independently pursue the Lord and seek to love him with their heart, soul, mind and strength, God draws them closer together as they draw closer to him. But all too often we seek to simply fix the other person with our own ideas of what needs to change and more often than not, we are left frustrated. The reasons for this are the true source of conflicts.

Conflict arises predominately from five different issues in relationships:

1. **Unmet expectations.** We all expect certain things from every relationship in our world. From spouses and family we expect support, time, affection, etc. Our expectations follow our perceptions of roles and boundaries we learned about in the last chapter. From neighbors we expect respect for boundaries, and behavior that fosters a peaceful social environment or acceptance of my socio-environmental impact. (Eg. I should be allowed to be the noisy neighbor!) From my employer I expect a good wage and achievable goals, as well as praise when I meet those goals. From my employee I expect good work done on time that benefits my bottom line. In nearly every conflict there are one or more individuals not meeting the expectations of others.

A Light Theology About Human Conflict

2. **Differing opinions.** Opinions are like armpits, we all have a couple and they all smell worse to everyone else than they do to ourselves. Conflict often arises when one or both people in a social relationship hold on tightly to their own opinions on an issue without compromise. Opinions usually lead to conflict because too many statements are being made and not enough questions are being asked. Opinions can change, but we seem to hold onto them too long.

3. **Lack of communication or miscommunication.** Many conflicts arise because someone either did not communicate information or feelings properly, or they did not communicate at all and the other person is left to fill in information gaps. Whenever we fill in gaps left by someone else, we tend to fill in those gaps in the way that we *perceive* things to be, which usually plays back into the problem of unmet expectations. Case in point: when someone asks you what you think about their idea or work, and you say it is fine, if they are insecure about the idea or work they will assume you are saying it is just okay, when in reality you may be saying it is fine in quality. An unspoken offense can occur in this moment through misinterpretation. We will talk about the importance of proper communication skills in a future chapter.

4. **Fatigue.** So many of our human conflicts happen during times of stress, hunger or sleep depravation. This is quite natural as these are the times where our self preservation instincts are at their peak. These are also the times when we tend to produce many more fruits of the flesh rather than fruits of the Spirit.

5. **Differing perspectives.** This may sound redundant as I have already mentioned differing opinions, but opinions and perspectives can be very different. Opinions tend to be something we adopt over time, and are based more on our belief system. Perspectives tend to be something that we inherit through our collected experiences and genetic makeup. This means that perspectives tend to be more difficult to let go of or change because they are rooted beyond our minds into our very DNA. As an example, if you grew up in an abusive home environment, then you are going to accept peoples intentions as good more slowly than someone who was raised in a more safe and secure environment. This is a natural perspective on human nature that needs time and new experiences to change. As a general rule, our opinions tend to flow out of our perspectives, and not the other way around. This means that sometimes to help change a poor opinion, we must first work at changing a flawed perspective.

A Light Theology About Human Conflict

However, this is not alway the case, which is why theology can be difficult. My perspective of God my be one of distrust due to past experiences, yet my opinion may be that God is sovereignly good, which can run in the opposite direction of my perspective.

In dealing with conflict, I cannot easily change your expectations, opinions, communication skills, fatigue level or perspectives on life. I can, however, look to God the author and finisher of my faith, and ask him to either change me, or give me the strength to love you with his love. This changes the approach in the relationship pyramid. (See the next diagram.)

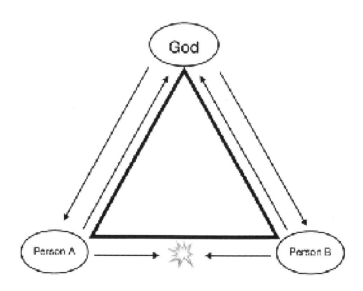

Peacemaking- Peacekeeping

There is a reason why Jesus said the two greatest commandments were to love God and love your neighbor (Matt. 22). The order was intentional! **We can not love our neighbor with genuineness until we first love God with our whole heart, soul, and mind. Genuine love flows from God.** When I pour my efforts into the most important relationship in my life, my God relationship, then God takes the fruit of that love and pours it out onto others. This allows me to approach the five sources of conflict in a different way from a different direction:

With unmet expectations, I can remember that my source of happiness and peace can not come from you, it must come from God. This allows me to find my fulfillment in Christ regardless of how you meet my expectations. This also allows me to stop wearing the weight of *your* expectations knowing that if I love God then he will use me to love you in the way that he deems necessary.

With differing opinions, I can begin to let go of the need to be heard because Jesus hears me and knows my heart. This allows me to start asking more questions about *your* opinions rather than feeling the need to be sure you hear my opinions.

With poor communication, I can begin to put into practice the Biblical principles of listening and

A Light Theology About Human Conflict

speaking that exudes the kindness and patience of Christ. This will begin to de-escalate rhetoric rather than escalating rhetoric.

With fatigue, I can begin to practice the fruit of the Spirit through the strength of the Spirit regardless of how I feel in the flesh.

With differing perspectives, I can be patient with the other person, asking the Lord to help me communicate truth to them in a way that will help them understand. We will talk in a future chapter about how this may come down to understanding perceptual modes.

When we place our God relationship above our human relationships, then the result will be what the rest of these verses talk about:

- **Vs 9 - We hold fast to good behaviors**

- **Vs 10 - We love with affection**

- **Vs 10 - We outdo the other person in showing honor and respect**

- **Vs 11 - We serve the other person with fervency and zeal**

- **Vs 12 - We find joy because of our hope in God**

- **Vs 13 - We have a patience in the troubled relationship**

- **Vs 13 - We are constantly praying for God's help**

- **Vs 14 - We are able to contribute to the needs of the other person and show them hospitality regardless of how we feel about them.**

Wisdom from Proverbs 10

Proverbs 10:11-13 (ESV)

"11 The mouth of the righteous is a fountain of life, but the mouth of the wicked conceals violence. 12 Hatred stirs up strife, but love covers all offenses. 13 On the lips of him who has understanding, wisdom is found, but a rod is for the back of him who lacks sense."

The way of love is to look for ways to respond with the kindness and patience of Christ. How many wars have started because no one wanted to be the one to let go of winning for the sake of peace?

Proverbs 10:18-21 (ESV)

"18 The one who conceals hatred has lying lips, and whoever utters slander is a fool. 19 When words are

A Light Theology About Human Conflict

many, transgression is not lacking, but whoever restrains his lips is prudent. 20 The tongue of the righteous is choice silver; the heart of the wicked is of little worth. 21 The lips of the righteous feed many, but fools die for lack of sense."

So many broken relationships could be averted if we would just slow down our speech and soften our tone.

Proverbs 10:29-32 (ESV)

"29 The way of the LORD is a stronghold to the blameless, but destruction to evildoers. 30 The righteous will never be removed, but the wicked will not dwell in the land. 31 The mouth of the righteous brings forth wisdom, but the perverse tongue will be cut off. 32 The lips of the righteous know what is acceptable, but the mouth of the wicked, what is perverse."

If God is for us, who can be against us? We don't have to defend our opinions and perspectives and expectations at all costs! God knows what we need before we have need of it (Matt. 6:8)! He will defend what he deems important!

Peacemaking - Peacekeeping

Let's look once again at what Pastor James said about conflict to the Jerusalem church:

James 1:19-27 (ESV)

19 Know this, my beloved brothers: let every person be quick to hear, slow to speak, slow to anger; 20 for the anger of man does not produce the righteousness of God. 21 Therefore put away all filthiness and rampant wickedness and receive with meekness the implanted word, which is able to save your souls. 22 But be doers of the word, and not hearers only, deceiving yourselves. 23 For if anyone is a hearer of the word and not a doer, he is like a man who looks intently at his natural face in a mirror. 24 For he looks at himself and goes away and at once forgets what he was like. 25 But the one who looks into the perfect law,

the law of liberty, and perseveres, being no hearer who forgets but a doer who acts, he will be blessed in his doing. 26 If anyone thinks he is religious and does not bridle his tongue but deceives his heart, this person's religion is worthless. 27 Religion that is pure and undefiled before God the Father is this: to visit orphans and widows in their affliction, and to keep oneself unstained from the world.

Prayer of Application - Reinhold Niebuhr's Prayer of Serenity: "God, grant me the serenity to accept the things I cannot change, courage to change the things I can, and wisdom to know the difference."

Chapter 4 - Pursuing Harmony When Peace Is Accomplishable

When I was a student in Bible college, I constantly heard preacher after preacher tell a story about an exchange between an aircraft carrier captain and a light house attendant. The story recapped a conversation in which the naval captain demanded the oncoming ship redirect their course, and the perceived captain of the other ship demanded the naval captain shift his own course. There was a back and forth, and a threat of destruction from the naval captain. The light house attendant finally revealed he was indeed manning a lowly lighthouse that could not move, and the naval captain finally redirected his course. The story, as it turns out, is not true and has been retold in various ways by various people for almost a hundred years. What strikes me is not how many times the story was told, but why so many preachers were telling the story to begin with. It is a great illustration of pride and conflict, but for me an even better illustration of how often we are dealing with pride and conflict among church members.

In this chapter, I want to transition now to a more practical and applicational teaching about dealing with conflicts, and I particularly want to focus over the next two chapters on the difference between peacemaking

A Light Theology About Human Conflict

and peacekeeping. Let's take a moment to review what we have learned to this point:

In chapter one I wanted us to understand how conflict brings division, but it can also bring connection! Human conflict can bring connection because it is intended to bring restoration. The conflict of the cross brought restoration to the garden relationship that God originally created and fostered with mankind!

In chapter two I pointed out how human conflicts can help define roles and boundaries. It must be stated that you will never learn to resolve human conflicts in your life until you resolve to learn the humility of Christ!

Chapter three was all about how human conflict defines true love. Human conflicts allow us to see and understand the true source of our love for others.

In this chapter I want to talk about how we pursue harmony in a conflicted relationship. Let's look now at the next few verses of Romans 12:

> Romans 12:14-18 (ESV)
>
> [14] Bless those who persecute you; bless and do not curse them. [15] Rejoice with those who rejoice, weep with those who weep. [16] Live in harmony with one another. Do not be haughty,

but associate with the lowly.
Never be wise in your own
sight. [17] Repay no one evil
for evil, but give thought to
do what is honorable in the
sight of all. [18] If possible, so
far as it depends on you,
live peaceably with all.

The English Standard Version uses the language of music in verse 16 when it says to live in harmony with one another. The KJV uses the phrase "Be of the same mind". The idea here is playing the same piece of music. I love that the ESV has chosen to translate this from a music perspective as I personally have witnessed and navigated many unnecessary conflicts in the church that began with a difference of opinion about music. The worship music wars of the 70's, 80's and 90's left a bad taste in my mouth for church as I watched two well intentioned sides lob insulting statements instead of asking sincere questions.

This whole passage gives the impression of making music from many parts of an orchestra and many different voices because all the instruments and voices are playing from the same sheet music. What is the sheet music that we play from? **The Gospel is our sheet music. If we are going to make much of the**

Gospel in a way that keeps us in unity, then we are going to have to be committed to peacemaking, not just peacekeeping.

Verse 18 is the key to this whole series. As far as it depends on us, we are to live peaceably with others. This means that sometimes we will be peacemakers, and sometimes we will be peacekeepers.

There is a huge difference between being a "peacemaker" and a "peacekeeper". The predominant difference is that peace makers are willing to deal with the issues. **Peacemaking is pursuing conversations with those we are in conflict with, with the goal of a restored and healthy relationship, while peacekeeping is doing what we can not to see more conflict stirred up.** Peacekeeping is necessary when only one person is willing to work at the relationship, or when two people in conflict are too vastly different to be in harmony without a major change in perspectives, opinions and expectations by both persons. (These kinds of relationships are often called toxic relationships.)

In an illustrative way: **Peacemaking is pursuing a fire to put it out, and peacekeeping is staying a safe distance from a fire with the effort of containing it to the damage already done.** Sometimes these fires burn themselves out and sometimes they burn to the end of days. There is a time and place for peacekeeping, but if there is hope and signs that restoration is possible, peacemaking honors the Lord and should be our ultimate goal.

Where does peacemaking start? Matthew 18 gives us the template for pursuing peace. In this passage, Jesus lays out a template for pursuing a brother or sister we are in conflict with. He gives four steps that we are to take in pursuing restoration:

Step 1 - Go to them alone and explain what it is you are concerned about or offended by (vs 15). This instruction is clear that the first person we have this conversation with is the person themselves. This does not mean we can not seek advice from others when we are trying to figure out how to start the conversation, but our intent should be to first contain the issue to the smallest circle as possible so that the fire of the conflict does not spread. Gossip is never an option. Keep in mind that if the purpose of Biblical confrontation is restoration (which it is!), then we must go with humility understanding that there may be faults we will need to admit and make right. If the person you are seeking to restore a relationship with is too arrogant to listen, then Jesus instructed us to move to the second step.

A Light Theology About Human Conflict

Step 2 - Go to them a second time with humble and Spiritual people that will help establish the truth (vs 16). Remember, if their job is to establish truth, they may realize in the course of the conversation that you may share in the problem for a particular reason. If you are not ready to receive truth in critique, then you are not yet ready to pursue restoration. If they still refuse to listen and work at the relationship, Jesus instructs us to move to step 3.

Step 3 - Get the church involved (vs 17). A few realities must be established to follow this step: First of all, this step really only works between two believers in community with one another. If the person you are in conflict with is an unbeliever, then this step will probably not work and may even damage the opportunity to share Christ with this person in the future. Secondly, if they are from another church, then two churches must be involved, not just your church. Thirdly, the "church" is not everyone in your church. Jesus is talking about wise leaders who will be able to lead you down a path of grace and humility in seeking restoration. Pastors, deacons, elders, teachers and so on are people who can be sought for help, but they need to be people who bring the strength of the church and the authority of the church into the issue. If you have involved the church leadership and the person continues to act in the same way, Jesus offers a fourth and final step.

Peacemaking - Peacekeeping

Step 4 - Create a safe boundary for peacekeeping (vs 18). Jesus explained that if they are not willing to humbly work at the relationship, that we are to act in such a way that the other person is a person who cannot be trusted. Jesus used the illustration of a "Gentile" or "tax collector". What Jesus is not saying is that we are to be cruel or unkind, or even that we are to write them off or dismiss them out of our lives. Jesus himself reached out to both Gentiles and tax collectors with love. Jesus is establishing the idea of healthy boundaries. An Israelite would not have trusted a Roman to come into their home and know all their business. They certainly would not have done that with a tax-collector. The point here is damage control and peace. This is the definition of peacekeeping that we have been looking at. Jesus is saying here that when a relationship is toxic and cannot be restored, we can be kind and gracious, and even loving by establishing healthy boundaries in the relationship until the other person has humbly offered to learn and grow to see the relationship restored. We will deal more with this situation in our final chapters.

At any point during steps 1 through 3, if the person we are in conflict with humbly responds with a desire to seek restoration, we are obligated by the love of Christ to pursue restoration. Sadly, we often do not pursue restoration because we do not really want it. The story of Jonah should remind us that God does not take this

A Light Theology About Human Conflict

lightly. God went to great lengths to get Jonah to pursue the people of Nineveh, the enemy of Israel. Pursuing someone who feels or behaves like an enemy can be very difficult. What we often fear the most is the initial conversation. Here are some important and practical tips on communicating with others during times of conflict.

"Do's" and "Do nots" of communication in conflict:

Do not speak in angry or annoyed tones. We tend to respond with a matching rhetoric and tone when it comes to communication. If you escalate rhetoric or tone, then the person you are speaking with will likely do the same. Proverbs 15:1 (ESV) states: "A soft answer turns away wrath, but a harsh word stirs up anger."

Do not resort to silence in tough situations. We are not always silent for wrong reasons. Sometimes we can not trust ourselves to have a soft response or to say things properly. In these moments we must seek God's wisdom through the Holy Spirit to have both the boldness and words we need. Remember James 1:5: we can seek wisdom from God, who will not withhold it. Often, however, silence is used as a tool of control or manipulation. We must check our own hearts and ask what our true intentions are.

Peacemaking - Peacekeeping

Do not speak in vague or general terms. Phrases and words like "I guess", "Maybe", "Fine" and "Whatever" do not communicate what is really on your heart. Be direct, but season your directness with kindness and grace. Matthew 5:37 (ESV) states: "Let what you say be simply 'yes' or 'no'; anything more than this comes from evil." Colossians 4:6 (ESV) states: "Let your speech always be gracious, seasoned with salt, so that you may know how you ought to answer each person."

Do not speak absolutely about non-absolutes. Statements like "You always" or "You never" are probably untrue and come off as harsh. For example: "You never listen to what I have to say" or "You always forget to acknowledge me" may feel accurate but are not precise and therefore cause the information you are trying to communicate to be "suspect". If what you are saying is true, then it is important to speak with precise truth wherever possible so that the information you are trying to communicate is not unduly questioned.

Do not contradict what you say by what you do. You cannot tell someone you care about them if you are not living a life of compassion and care. This will be seen as dishonesty. If you tell someone you desire to live in a healthy relationship with them, then you must put into practice the concepts of Romans 12:9-13 that I outlined in the last chapter.

A Light Theology About Human Conflict

Do not initiate important discussions at inconvenient or constrained times. Ten minutes before church starts or in the middle of a church fellowship is not a time to throw out a statement of contention. (People sometimes do this so that they will not have to answer for their own attitude or actions. This is far from kind!) Email, phone calls, texts, instant messages are never the best way to confront a brother or sister. Face to face with soft tones and sincere expressions is always the best way. Sometimes we must resort to other forms of communication, but this should be the exception, not the rule! I once saw a highway billboard rented by a man asking his wife for a divorce. This is an extreme example of what can happen when a relationship is so neglected and broken.

Do focus and give individual attention when communicating and keep your body language in mind. Confrontation should not be multitasked. Confrontation and restorative conversations should be handled with great care. If the conversation is important, then it should receive the prioritization of your focus. It can be very difficult to look at someone in the eyes and speak to them when you are angry at them or hurt by them. If you can muster the courage, it is important because the eyes really are the window to the soul and communicate your sincerity. You may not always have the courage to look someone in the eye, but it is important that you do not communicate through your body language that this conversation is unimportant. If the conversation is unimportant, then the relationship is unimportant. Parents, this is imperative when it comes to difficult conversations with our children. Spouses, this is important in our marriage conflicts.

Do ask clear and direct questions without hidden agendas, that take into consideration perceptual modes. Questions are always better than statements for a number of reasons:

- Questions allow you to listen and learn better what the other person is truly frustrated with.

- Questions communicate to the other person that you are not stubborn or arrogant, but that you sincerely want to understand.

- Questions allow for a two way conversation (or dialogue) rather than two one-way monologues.

Perceptual modes are the way we communicate and receive information. (Dr. H. Norman Wright gives a great synopsis of this concept in his book *Now That You Are Engaged*, Regal Books, page 140-141. Much of my understanding of these concepts comes from his material.)

A Light Theology About Human Conflict

Visual based communicators need to see things to understand. They predominantly understand and explain things with visual or physical ideas and illustrations. These types of people need you to patiently *show* *them* what it is you are trying to communicate. Give visible examples and illustrations. Questions like: "Do you see what I am trying to explain?" or "How can I help you see this about me?" may help communicate better.

Auditory based communicators use words purposefully and in great volume. They do not mind talking through an issue, but require open and well-formed dialogue. These types of people need ample time to discuss and understand the issues in a given conflict. Questions like: "Do you understand what I am trying to say?" or "Am I making myself clear?" can be helpful questions.

Feelings based communicators filter information by how they feel emotionally or what they can sense. Special care must be taken to be sensitive to tone of voice and rhetoric as these types of people will tend to be more sensitive. A visual or auditory person will tend to struggle with what cannot be qualified or quantified in this persons feelings, but their feelings should not be dismissed without patient and gracious dialogue and effort to understand. Questions like: "How do you feel

about that?" or "I am getting the sense you think
_____, am I right?"

Remember that direct questions will often cause healthier communication than direct statements. Some more examples of good questions:

- I am hearing you say _____, is that what you mean to say?

- When I say _____, what do you feel, or think I am really saying?

- When I react in _____ way, do you think I am angry with you?

- Do you see what I am trying to show you, or hear what I am trying to communicate?

- Why did you respond with _____ in that moment or after I said that?

- Can you help me understand what it is you want me to see or hear?

- When I did or said _____, what did you feel in that moment?

Once again, let us turn our attention to the wisdom of Proverbs:

A Light Theology About Human Conflict

Proverbs 12:16-20 (ESV)

"16 The vexation of a fool is known at once, but the prudent ignores an insult. 17 Whoever speaks the truth gives honest evidence, but a false witness utters deceit. 18 There is one whose rash words are like sword thrusts, but the tongue of the wise brings healing. 19 Truthful lips endure forever, but a lying tongue is but for a moment. 20 Deceit is in the heart of those who devise evil, but those who plan peace have joy."

You can see in this passage the concepts of both peacemaking and peacekeeping. I have found with certain people that I must steer clear and keep my speech to a minimum. Proverbs calls these people either scoffers or fools! These people will not receive truth and wisdom, but will take my words and twist them for ungodly reasons. With others, the task of speaking truth may be difficult, but it is necessary and has been placed in our hearts by the Holy Spirit for the purpose of restoration for God's glory. We need to be humble and sensitive to the Holy Spirit if we are going to know the difference.

Peacemaking - Peacekeeping

Look once again at what Pastor James said about conflict to the Jerusalem church:

> James 3:1-12 (ESV)
>
> [1] Not many of you should become teachers, my brothers, for you know that we who teach will be judged with greater strictness. [2] For we all stumble in many ways. And if anyone does not stumble in what he says, he is a perfect man, able also to bridle his whole body. [3] If we put bits into the mouths of horses so that they obey us, we guide their whole bodies as well. [4] Look at the ships also: though they are so large and are driven by strong winds, they are guided by a very small rudder wherever the will of the pilot directs. [5] So also the tongue is a small member, yet it boasts of great things. How great a forest is set ablaze by such

A Light Theology About Human Conflict

a small fire! 6 And the tongue
is a fire, a world of
unrighteousness. The
tongue is set among our
members, staining the
whole body, setting on fire
the entire course of life, and
set on fire by hell. 7 For
every kind of beast and
bird, of reptile and sea
creature, can be tamed and
has been tamed by
mankind, 8 but no human
being can tame the tongue.
It is a restless evil, full of
deadly poison. 9 With it we
bless our Lord and Father,
and with it we curse people
who are made in the
likeness of God. 10 From the
same mouth come blessing
and cursing. My brothers,
these things ought not to be
so. 11 Does a spring pour
forth from the same opening
both fresh and salt water?
12 Can a fig tree, my
brothers, bear olives, or a

Peacemaking - Peacekeeping

grapevine produce figs?
Neither can a salt pond
yield fresh water.

I once sat with a dear friend and we wept together as his wife had cheated on him, divorced him and taken their daughter. In brokenness he asked how he would ever be able to show her the love of Christ. What the Lord laid on my heart to say in that moment has come to me again and again in many difficult broken relationships that I have had to counsel people through over my ministry career. I instructed my friend to pray, and to start with a prayer for pity. When God sees our sinful condition, he does not *only* feel angry for what sin has done, he also feels pity for us and our condition. It saddens the Father to see what his children have done to their lives. Matthew 9 tells us that when Jesus saw the crowds of people, he felt compassion because he pitied them as sheep needing a shepherd. To feel compassion, or passionate love, we must first pity the great need of that person. The following prayer is a prayer of levels and stages that may take years to see answered in any way. The first step is the most difficult, and begins with pity, but can lead in God's time and way to peace.

Once I pity someone I can begin to see their neediness. This God given perspective will allow me to ask how I may help to meet that need. I may not be able to meet it directly, but now I can at least begin to pray that God would meet that need in a way that they might see His faithfulness. Once I feel a sense of passion in sincere Godly love, then I will begin to ask God how I may pursue them with that love. This may mean in the simplest way not wishing ill upon them. This may mean reaching out to actually find an amicable understanding or agreement to live in the same community without unkindness. The Lord will lead in those directives.

Once I am able to pursue kindness, then it is important for me to continually practice the fruits of the Spirit, regardless of who they are and how they act. The practice of being in the Spirit's leading will allow me to have peace that I have done my part to heal the relationship and the rest of the work belongs to them. Again, all of this begins with a prayer for pity.

Prayer of Application - The Prayer for Peace: "Lord, Give me Pity that becomes Passion, Passion that results in Pursuit, Pursuit that continues in Persistence, Persistence that turns into Practice, and Practice that results in Peace."

Chapter 5 - Heaping Coals When Peace Seems Un-accomplishable

In Centralia, Pennsylvania a coal mine fire has existed since the 1960's. This town that once had around 1500 residents left over from the peak years of the coal mining industry now boasts a meager 7 residents as most of the town is un-inhabitable. The fire started when the town decided it did not want to deal with its growing collection of trash at illegal dumpsites due to the cost. They decided to collect the trash and light it on fire not realizing it was being collected over top of an exposed coal seam. The fire began to spread under the earth as the town council argued over cost and blame. Because of the amount of time it took to work through the conflict, the fire is now uncontainable and is projected to burn for the next 250 years. This fire serves as a physical illustration of people not wanting to deal with problems, and not working through conflict in a healthy way. Now the fire that has resulted must burn itself out and the people that once lived in Centralia have had to move on in order to live in peace.

In this chapter I want to conclude this very light theology on conflict with the sometimes necessary pursuit of peacekeeping as opposed to peacemaking. We will merely scratch the surface and if I am honest, might bring up more questions than answers.

A Light Theology About Human Conflict

If I accomplish nothing else other than getting us to slow down and seek the Lord's wisdom through the Holy Spirit during times of human conflict, then I still believe I will have accomplished a necessary mission. Too many times we are flying into conflict without wisdom, or flying away from conflict without courage. Both peacemaking and peacekeeping require a sensitivity to the Lord and a willingness to do neither more nor less than what He is leading us to do.

As we begin the study of peacekeeping, I want to put all our previous chapters together to connect all their truths like links in a chain to help us understand how we come to peacekeeping as a final reality in a broken relationship.

In chapter one I discussed how conflict brings division, but it can also bring connection! Human conflict can bring connection because it is intended to bring restoration.   The conflict of the cross brought restoration to the garden relationship God originally created and fostered with mankind!

In chapter two I pointed out how human conflicts can help define roles and boundaries. We must remember that we will never learn to resolve human conflicts in our lives until we resolve to learn the humility of Christ!

In chapter three we were reminded that human conflict defines true love in that it allows us to see and understand the true source of our love for others. Our love must first flow toward God and then from God to others. The order is important! If we don't love God with our heart, soul and mind, we will not love our neighbor.

In chapter four we learned that we must pursue harmony when peace is accomplishable and our harmony revolves around the Gospel! If we are going to make much of the Gospel in a way that keeps us in unity, then we are going to have to be committed to peacemaking, not just peacekeeping. Peacemaking is pursuing conversations with those we are in conflict with, with the goal of a restored and healthy relationship, while peacekeeping is doing what we can not to see more conflict stirred up. Peacemaking is pursuing a fire to put it out, and peacekeeping is staying a safe distance from a fire with the effort of containing it to the damage already done.

In this final chapter, I want to discuss the following question: **What do we do when we are not able to restore a broken relationship?**

I want to start to answer this question by finishing our passage in Romans 12.

> Romans 12:18-21 (ESV)
>
> 18 If possible, so far as it depends on you, live peaceably with all.

A Light Theology About Human Conflict

19 Beloved, never avenge
yourselves, but leave it to
the wrath of God, for it is
written, "Vengeance is mine,
I will repay, says the Lord."
20 To the contrary, "if your
enemy is hungry, feed him;
if he is thirsty, give him
something to drink; for by
so doing you will heap
burning coals on his head."
21 Do not be overcome by
evil, but overcome evil with
good.

Verse 18 pivots between "peacemaking" and "peacekeeping". Again, at the risk of sounding redundant, peacemaking is pursuing conversations with those we are in conflict with, with the goal of a restored and healthy relationship, while peacekeeping is doing what we can not to see more conflict stirred up. Peacemaking is pursuing a fire to put it out, and peacekeeping is staying a safe distance from a fire with the effort of containing it to the damage already done.

Just as there is a difference between peacemaking and peacekeeping, there is also an important difference between peacekeeping and appeasement. I once

Peacemaking - Peacekeeping

heard R. C. Sproul say that we need to not mistake keeping the peace for appeasement in addressing our culture. The same is true for personal conflicts, especially with people who are abusive and vindictive. It is not loving as Christ loves to let someone get away with unkindness un-confronted. Jesus Christ was loving and still directly addressed the sin of the people he was loving. One of the most loving things we can do is to tell someone they are being unloving. We can tell someone they are unloving, lovingly! (Remember the do's and do not's of communication discussed in the last chapter.)

Remember, peacekeeping is about not adding fuel to the fire, it does not mean we do not fight the fire. We must fight fire with water, and sometimes even with fire if we are going to do damage control. We do not toss in fuel!

One way to evaluate if our hearts are pure in directly confronting abuse is to evaluate what damage or injustice may occur if we do nothing. It is possible that we may stop the abuse of others by dealing with the abuse that is happening to us. Physical and emotional abuse should never be tolerated and when possible should be addressed directly and called out as sin. Sometimes for safety reasons we have to simply escape the relationship in its current form. This is

A Light Theology About Human Conflict

where it is important to lean on the support and help of the "others" Jesus spoke about in Matthew 18.

Remarkably, the Bible seems to connect human conflict and confrontation to the number "18". Out of this has come for me what I like to call "the 18 plan".

Remember the "18" plan:

Matthew 18 is the peacekeeping mission; know the steps of confrontation and understand your boundaries.

Proverbs 18:12 says "Before destruction a man's heart is haughty, but humility comes before honor." This reminds us that we need humility to do this right.

Romans 12:18 says "If possible, so far as it depends on you, live peaceably with all." This reminds us that we can be peaceful regardless of what others do.

James 3:18 says "A harvest of righteousness is sown in peace by those who make peace." If God gives you the opportunity, make peace, do not just keep the peace.

Peacemaking- Peacekeeping

In Romans 12, Paul gives us a very good example of what it looks like to be caught up in our own emotion of anger and vengeance. There is much more to this verse than how we read it. The verse states: "Beloved, never avenge yourselves, but leave it to the wrath of God, for it is written, 'Vengeance is mine, I will repay, says the Lord.'" Paul is quoting Deuteronomy 32:35. The context behind this verse is very important. This verse is part of a larger Psalm that Moses wrote and gave to the people at the conclusion of giving the law. It is a warning that God is both loving and jealous, and will do whatever is necessary to hold on to His people in covenant relationship. Look at the verse in context:

Deuteronomy 32:34-38 (ESV)

18 If possible, so far as it depends on you, live peaceably with all. 34 "'Is not this laid up in store with me, sealed up in my treasuries? 35 Vengeance is mine, and recompense, for the time when their foot shall slip; for the day of their calamity is at hand, and their doom comes swiftly.' 36 For the LORD will vindicate his people and

> have compassion on his
> servants, when he sees that
> their power is gone and
> there is none remaining,
> bond or free. 37 Then he will
> say, 'Where are their gods,
> the rock in which they took
> refuge, 38 who ate the fat of
> their sacrifices and drank
> the wine of their drink
> offering? Let them rise up
> and help you; let them be
> your protection!"

Moses wanted Israel to see the theology of God's covenant faithfulness manifested through the confrontation of their sinfulness. Here is the great irony of this chapter: in the next few verses of Deuteronomy 32, God reminds Moses that he (Moses) will be laid to rest on a mountain outside of the promised land for "breaking faith" with Yahweh. This happened at a time of great frustration for Moses when at the rock called Meribah-kadesh God asked Moses to speak to the rock and call forth water. Moses was so frustrated with the constant complaining of the people, that he smote the rock with his staff instead. In this simple act of anger, he took on the jealous rage that rightfully belonged to God and made it his own. It was an act of pride and arrogance that placed Moses in the position of God. Moses made God's righteous and justified anger his own, and responded with sinful anger when God was actually showing mercy. God said that this was the same as breaking faith with Him.

The implications on Romans 12 are staggering. **It takes real faith to trust God with those relationships we can not mend! It takes real faith to hold our tongue and keep our anger in check. Romans 12:19 reminds us that no broken relationship is outside the sovereign power and authority of God. God is always doing a work in every human conflict.**

God uses mended relationships and the renewing of vows, but He also must use divorce. God must use the mess that is humanity, for He sent His only begotten Son into the mess to redeem humanity. It takes real faith to trust that God is bigger than our frail and fractured human relationships.

Paul wrapped up this section of teaching about human relationships and conflicts with an analogy of burning coals. Paul, just as James, saw the idea of fire as a proper illustration of human conflict. Paul instructed the believer to heap burning coals onto the hearth of those who refuse to deal with and work through their own issues that cause conflict with others. Paul is instructing us to respond to broken relationships in

A Light Theology About Human Conflict

such a way that we allow the other person to deal with the fire they are continuing to ignite or allowing to burn. Coach Tony Dungy wrote a book called *Quiet Strength*. In that book he talked about teaching his players to understand the difference between reacting and responding both on the football field, and in life. I have drawn upon this truth in many ways throughout my years of dealing with conflicts in ministry. Heaping coals defines the difference between responding and reacting.

Here are some things I have seen as differences between responding and reacting.

- **Responding is rooted in the Holy Spirit, while reacting is rooted in the flesh.**

In another letter to the Galatian church (chapter 5), Paul speaks of walking in step with the Holy Spirit. In this analogous teaching Paul gives a comparison of responses ,or fruits, that come from the Spirit of God, and reactions ,or fruits, that come from our flesh. The fruit of the flesh is a dark opposite of the fruit of the Spirit. The fruit of the Spirit is love, joy, peace, patience, kindness, goodness, faithfulness, gentleness, and self-control. It is not only accomplishable, but even expected by God that when we are relegated to the task of peacekeeping instead of peacemaking, that we will still reflect the Holy Spirit with character qualities such as these. Any one of these fruits can be exercised in silence when necessary.

- **Responding draws from wisdom, while reacting draws purely from emotion.**

Again, Pastor James reminds us in James 1:5 that we can ask for wisdom. Learn the power of the pause! Learn not to speak until spoken to....by the Holy Spirit of God or through God's Word. James also reminded us in James 1:19 that we are to be quick to hear, slow to speak and slow to get angry. If you want to control a conversation, the best thing to do is to be in control of your emotions. When we are dealing with people who only want to win a fight and do not want to deal with their own issues, they will do everything in their power to make us look angry and unstable. Do not give them this weapon! It is perfectly okay to be quiet until we are composed, or to inform the individual we need time to pray and formulate a response.

- **Responding asks questions, while reacting makes statements.**

We have already discussed this in some detail. Whether peacemaking or peacekeeping, this concept holds true.

- **Responding softens our answer, while reacting enflames our answer.**

A Light Theology About Human Conflict

If we are yielded to the Holy Spirit as Galatians 5 states, then we will not say more or less than the Spirit gives us to say. We will not run ahead or lag behind the Holy Spirit's leading. In doing this, our tone and temper will be what the Holy Spirit wants it to be to properly communicate truth. If we fail in this effort, all is not lost. The Holy Spirit can mightily use a humble apology for fleshly fruit just as much as he can use the perfect response. The reality is, we will rarely if ever nail every confrontation or response to provocation with the perfect response. God knows this, and it is precisely why He gave us the Holy Spirit and the Word of God.

- **Responding often takes time, while reacting usually answers immediately.**

Again, learn the power of the pause. Also, be committed to long term relationship rebuilding. Most broken relationships happen over time, so do not expect that you are going to fix the issue with one magical phrase. Usually what is on the tip of our tongue is born of pent up frustration that we are just wanting to release. We need to give ourselves the gift of time to listen to the Holy Spirit and search the Word of God.

- **Responding desires to establish truth, while reacting desires to prove a point.**

Peacemaking - Peacekeeping

We must check the motives of our hearts because truth needs no defense. Whether truth is proven to a skeptic or not, it remains true. Sometimes as peacekeepers, we have to be willing to let go of the acknowledgment that we are right. If we have established truth, especially with witnesses, then we must lovingly allow the other person to be wrong and pray that they recognize truth before the lies destroy them.

- **Responding desires to show God's consistent and faithful love, while reacting desires to establish rights.**

Above all, our desire in peacekeeping should be to exhibit the peace of Christ so that the other person can begin to see what it is like to live without peace, especially if the other person is involved in sinful attitudes and actions. That is why Paul follows up the concept of "heaping coals" with showing love and generosity. This allows the other person to be alone with the fire as they see your health and healing.

- **Responding looks like Philippians 2, while reacting looks like James 4.**

Philippians chapter two speaks of the humility Christ exhibited in coming to this earth. Jesus Christ had a claim to the throne with all the rights that came with that throne, yet he chose to enter the world in lowly

A Light Theology About Human Conflict

esteem and take on a criminals cross that we might be reconciled to God. Responding looks like strategic sacrifice for the sake of restoration. James 4 speaks of the source of quarrels and fights: our own selfish passions and desires.

Once again, we turn to the wisdom of Solomon to his sons in dealing with conflict. The following Proverbs speak to the process of peacekeeping.

Proverbs 12:15 (ESV)

The way of a fool is right in his own eyes, but a wise man listens to advice.

There is no point in trying to argue someone into truth, especially if they are never willing to acknowledge they might be wrong. I have heard it said that the definition of insanity is doing the same thing over and over again and getting the same result. This sounds just like arguing with a fool to me!

Proverbs 18:1-2 (ESV)

[1] Whoever isolates himself seeks his own desire; he breaks out against all sound judgment. [2] A fool takes no pleasure in understanding, but only in expressing his opinion.

Peacemaking - Peacekeeping

You can not argue with a fool, so it does no good to try. Do not waste any more time until they indicate they are willing to listen.

Proverbs 18:6-8 (ESV)

6 A fool's lips walk into a fight, and his mouth invites a beating. 7 A fool's mouth is his ruin, and his lips are a snare to his soul. 8 The words of a whisperer are like delicious morsels; they go down into the inner parts of the body.

Do not try to counteract a fool by acting like a fool. We do this by either arguing with them, or giving them more time and a listening ear to do more damage.

Proverbs 18:19-21 (ESV)

19 A brother offended is more unyielding than a strong city, and quarreling is like the bars of a castle. 20 From the fruit of a man's mouth his stomach is satisfied; he is satisfied by the yield of his lips. 21 Death and life are in the power of the tongue, and those who love it will eat its fruits.

If someone is unwilling to let go of their bitterness, you will spend a lot of time, energy and resources trying to break down the castle of their bitterness. Wait until they open the gates of their heart in humility and sincerity! When we try to force an issue we risk

A Light Theology About Human Conflict

entering the prison of bitterness ourselves when we do not get the answer or results we desire.

Proverbs 26:4-5 (ESV)

4 Answer not a fool according to his folly, lest you be like him yourself. 5 Answer a fool according to his folly, lest he be wise in his own eyes.

This verse can seem contradictory, but it is presenting 2 scenarios:

- With a fool unwilling to listen and reconcile, it is foolish to continue to try.

- When there is hope that a fool might listen, give them the hard grace of telling them the truth. (This goes back to the Matthew 18 process of confrontation.)

Proverbs 26:17-19 (ESV)

17 Whoever meddles in a quarrel not his own is like one who takes a passing dog by the ears. 18 Like a madman who throws firebrands, arrows, and death 19 is the man who deceives his neighbor and says, "I am only joking!"

Stay out of conflict that is not God given! You do not need more conflict than you already have. Sometimes this means adding more conflict to an already conflicted relationship. Also, do not use sarcasm as a weapon! You are not joking, you are being passive aggressive, which is cowardly! Be courageously and graciously direct.

Proverbs 26:20-22 (ESV)

20 For lack of wood the fire goes out, and where there is no whisperer, quarreling ceases. 21 As charcoal to hot embers and wood to fire, so is a quarrelsome man for kindling strife. 22 The words of a whisperer are like delicious morsels; they go down into the inner parts of the body.

When we heap burning coals, we are not adding more coal. We are pushing coals into the corner of the one who does not want them to burn out. We are allowing them to deal with the consequences. Bitterness holds us in the furnace of self consumption. Bitterness will eventually burn out other healthy relationships and even the physical health of our bodies.

As we have done in every chapter, I would like to close this chapter with scripture and prayer. The prayer, you will notice, is the same prayer I gave in the last chapter. My hope is that you can continue on the path of prayer toward self healing and peace, or a healed relationship with the person you are in conflict with. Remember, the goal is to see God do a work in us, regardless of what he does with the relationship. If God must use a broken relationship to put us on the path of healing our relationship with him, then that is exactly what he will

A Light Theology About Human Conflict

use. This portion of James I referred to earlier is an indictment on those with whom we cannot make peace, but it is also a reminder to us who are seeking to honor the Lord, not to become like them as we endeavor to keep the peace.

James 4:1-11 (ESV)

[1] What causes quarrels and what causes fights among you? Is it not this, that your passions are at war within you? [2] You desire and do not have, so you murder. You covet and cannot obtain, so you fight and quarrel. You do not have, because you do not ask. [3] You ask and do not receive, because you ask wrongly, to spend it on your passions. [4] You adulterous people! Do you not know that friendship with the world is enmity with God? Therefore whoever wishes to be a friend of the world makes himself an enemy of God. [5] Or do you suppose it is to no purpose

that the Scripture says, "He yearns jealously over the spirit that he has made to dwell in us"? 6 But he gives more grace. Therefore it says, "God opposes the proud but gives grace to the humble." 7 Submit yourselves therefore to God. Resist the devil, and he will flee from you. 8 Draw near to God, and he will draw near to you. Cleanse your hands, you sinners, and purify your hearts, you double-minded. 9 Be wretched and mourn and weep. Let your laughter be turned to mourning and your joy to gloom. 10 Humble yourselves before the Lord, and he will exalt you. 11 Do not speak evil against one another, brothers. The one who speaks against a brother or judges his brother, speaks evil against the law and judges the law. But if you judge the law, you

are not a doer of the law but
a judge. [12] There is only one
lawgiver and judge, he who
is able to save and to
destroy. But who are you to
judge your neighbor?

The Prayer of Peace: "Lord, Give me Pity that becomes Passion, Passion that results in Pursuit, Pursuit that continues in Persistence, Persistence that turns into Practice, and Practice that results in Peace."

In Conclusion - The Long Investment

A number of years ago a business man stepped in to help me and my wife out of a difficult financial situation. My wife and I conceived our first child before we were ready financially or had sufficient health insurance. Although we were overjoyed by the news of our growing family, it began a vicious cycle of financial struggle for us that lasted about a decade until this man graciously stepped in and helped us get everything sorted out. One of the things he did was give me $500 dollars to open an investment account in order to teach me about the stock market and long term investing. I have never been endowed with the gift of finding money, and as of today over a decade later that fund is worth about $485. There was a point at which it was worth almost double. The real lesson here and the point the wise man was trying to help me see was the impatience we often struggle with when it comes to spending or investing money. If you are not committed to long term patience in investing then you will probably not see a substantial return on your investments. Human relationships are very similar. As conflicts arise we must often practice patience instead of withdrawal, understanding that it may be months or years before we see the relationship improve and increase.

A Light Theology About Human Conflict

Healthy relationships are a long term investment. Some conflicted relationships are going to take a life time of commitment to see God do real work and some will never be restored on this side of death. We can never judge in our human lifetime what a relationship has brought to our lives. Even the most conflicted relationships are teaching us about our own character quality and weaknesses and allowing us the invaluable opportunity to grow and change as people.

The book of Acts records a famous human conflict involving the very apostle we have gleaned so much wisdom from in this book. The apostle Paul had a relational conflict that as far as we are told, was never resolved.

In the larger context of Acts 15, the apostles were trying to bring the early church together in unity and out of the constant struggle the Jewish and Gentile believers had to understand and support one another. The church was an eclectic group of people all trying to work out of their own opinions and perspectives (remember the difference from previous chapters) and come together in the harmony of the Gospel. **Still today, the church is constantly learning how to work through conflicts built on opinions and perspectives.** The big thing to notice is that there was a willingness to love sacrificially. The Jews would be patient with the Gentiles in not holding them to the traditional law.   The Gentiles would not flaunt their liberty by brining meat offered to idols into the church feasts and partaking in the sexually immoral practices of the Gentile cultures. What is so amazing about this chapter in Acts is that even though the Apostle Paul is trying to help the church work through conflict, the chapter ends with the story of Paul's own conflict with a fellow church leader.

The apostle Paul started life in a very different way than he ended it. Born a Jewish Roman citizen, he was very privileged in his educational upbringing. He studied the law under a famous Jewish Rabbi named Gamaliel. His education would have been an Ivy-League education today. He landed an authoritative position in the upper levels of Jewish society and was deputized to deal with the crazy Christians who were drawing people away from Judaism. During one such mission Jesus Christ appeared to Paul in a blinding light and confronted him. Paul wisely surrendered his life to Jesus. What followed was a messy process of working through trust layers in the church and being discipled to understand the freedom Christ offers from the Law of Moses. Enter Barnabas. Barnabas, whose name means "son of encouragement" invested greatly into Paul and became both a friend and ministry partner to Paul. In due course, Paul adopted a young apprentice for discipleship named John Mark. On one particular mission journey that must have been a fairly difficult

A Light Theology About Human Conflict

experience, John Mark left and went home. This angered Paul fiercely to the point that he refused to work with him any more. Barnabas felt that John Mark needed another chance to grow but Paul would have none of it. There arose such a sharp contention between them that they went their separate ways and no longer worked together (Acts 15:36-41).

Paul and Barnabas' struggle to come together on the issue of John Mark can serve as an important and encouraging test case for us as believers and we can learn both from what we do not know about the situation as well as what we do know.

Here is what we do not know:

We do not know who was right or wrong and that should remind us to be humble!

We often look at establishing truth in conflict with one another with the view of a coin. One side of the coin is heads, and one side is tails. If we can not establish truth we are even tempted to flip the coin and let it land where it will to determine who is right. The reality is that there is not only two sides to a coin, there are actually three sides to a coin! There is also that third very tiny outside edge of the coin where heads meets tails. I propose that in many conflicts this tiny edge is where the truth resides. It is very important if we find ourselves in the unwanted role of being a Matthew 18 mediator that we do not rush to judgment on who is right or wrong. Often, if not most of the time, both parties in a relational conflict possess a bit of truth as well as part of the blame. We need the Holy Spirit to point out the weaknesses in both parties that must change in order for the relationship to be restored to unity.

In this particular situation, Paul may have been correct that John Mark, due to his track record, would not be a wise choice for the next mission, but could Paul have trusted Barnabas' discretion? Barnabas was committed to seeing his young cousin (Col. 4:10 tells us they were related) grow in his faith, but was his commitment so strong that it clouded his judgement? Perhaps neither, perhaps both, we need the Lord's wisdom to know what is true in these situations.

We do not know if they ever completely reconciled and that should give us hope.

Think of this: the very man who instructs us in Romans 12 to live in harmony with others can not live in harmony with the very man who discipled him! I do not bring this up to defame Paul. Paul did learn, and in fact at the end of his days called for John Mark to come aid him in ministry (2 Timothy 4). I bring this up because if Paul can struggle with human conflict resolution and still be used of the Lord in such long

A Light Theology About Human Conflict

lasting and profound ways, then there is hope for you and I as well.

Here is what we do know:

We do know that Paul and Barnabas broadened their scope of ministry by going different directions and reaching different people groups.

Did you ever consider the reality that God can and will use church splits for His glory through the furtherance of the Gospel? I am as guilty as anyone of pointing out the tragedy of churches splitting over petty issues, and it is truly a tragedy as it communicates the hard truth that Christians are humans that struggle with love just like the rest of the world. But in reality, if both groups are able to recover and learn then we have just allowed for more influence in this world. I do not think this is the best way to advance the Gospel, or even a good way, but God can only use brokenness to reach this world because broken is what we are. I love to watch healthy churches send a group out in a healthy way to plant more healthy churches, but the reality is that more churches are started through brokenness these days than through healthy missional planning. God still sits on his throne and will use these situations for his good, glory and the advancement of the Gospel message.

Peacemaking - Peacekeeping

We do know that Paul and Barnabas were able to maintain a respect for one another that was cordial.

In 1 Corinthians 9:6 Paul mentions Barnabas as a co-laborer. Again, we do not know if they reconciled, but if they did not fully reconcile then this is a good example of peacekeeping and heaping coals.

We do know that God used Barnabas's discipleship of John Mark to bring him into a healthy place of ministry. Without the conflict, this may not have happened.

In Colossians 4:10 we see that Paul eventually requested John Mark's presence. This tells us with certainty that Paul at least was able to reconcile with John Mark.

In 2 Timothy 4:11 Paul not only requested the presence of John Mark, but even stated that he was very useful to him for ministry! This tells us that Barnabas must have done a great job of discipling him through his immaturity as a minister of the Gospel and helped him overcome his faith struggles.

There really are relationships that will not be restored on this earth. God used Paul and Barnabas in their broken relationship to double their missions efforts. God can, will and must use broken relationships because we are broken people that He can and wants to restore. God only has brokenness to work with

A Light Theology About Human Conflict

because sin has broken everything. If you are going to make a long term investment into a relationship, you are going to have to have a vision for rebuilding!

Nowhere is long term commitment more visible than in marriage.

Much of what I deal with as a pastor in counseling is conflict resolution. Most of the conflict resolution I deal with is in marriage. Much of the material I have put forward in this book comes from my own years of marriage and pre-marriage counseling. Some comes from personal experience, as I have seen my own fair share of human conflicts.

There is an ebb and flow to every human relationship. Every relationship is susceptible to brokenness and must receive the care necessary to keep it healthy. The marriage relationship, above all, is supremely important because (as Paul states in Ephesians) it is a picture of the relationship we have with God in his restorative pursuit of us. The true goal of the marriage relationship is to pursue the same type of closeness in harmony that God pursues with us. The reality is that the marriage relationship is under attack constantly due to the pressures and stresses of life.

Peacemaking - Peacekeeping

I would like to offer one last bit of instruction regarding human conflicts as pertains to marriage as many reading this book will be dealing with conflicts in marriage. Allow me to illustrate what I want to write about with another relationship pyramid.

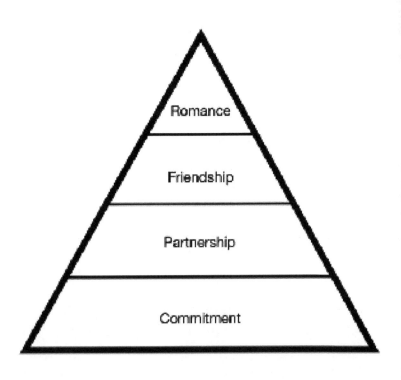

Truth be told, this relationship pyramid could be used as an illustration of any type of relationship as the word "Romance" could be replaced with other words that describe the ideal notions of what a relationship is

A Light Theology About Human Conflict

supposed to be.   I designed this pyramid to best describe marriage.

My wife and I went on a cruise for our honeymoon and found ourselves at a Mayan pyramid during one port of call.   It was an amazing sight to see the construction and think of what it must have taken thousands of years ago to build such a structure.   I am sure the Mayan pyramids pale in comparison to the Egyptian pyramids, which I have never had the privilege to see up to this point.   If you are like me, when I look at pyramids whether in pictures or in real life, your eyes are drawn to the top, the pinnacle.   There is a beauty in the geometry and architecture.

Romance in a relationship is very similar.   We read books about romance.   We write songs about romance.   We make movies about romance.   We usually fall in love because of romance!

As a pyramid weathers and erodes, one of the first parts of the pyramid to change in shape and sharpness is the top.   As the top erodes due to wind or weather, the pyramid becomes shorter and less attractive over time.   In relationships, one of the first things to erode is the romance.   For many couples this happens over years, for some right after the honeymoon.   Many pressures and stresses can cause the romance to fade and not every marriage will face the same struggles, but in most marriages the romance will certainly fade to some degree.

A pyramid without a peak is still a pyramid, and still a wonder to behold. A marriage without romance can still be wonderful as well, because there is still much to the structure, but as romance fades, friendship becomes the peak.

My wife and I were best friends who fell in love, so we have been able to appreciate the friendship focus that we have. (We sill enjoy and long for romance!) Friendship is a settled stage for many married couples. They are content, especially through the busy stages of raising a family, to enjoy the comforts that a good friendship provides. The difficult reality for many couples is that the friendship can fade as well.

When it is your turn to get up and deal with the needs of a child at 3AM in the morning, that friend in your bed can feel like an enemy. For many couples, the friendship may fade as well, and the pinnacle of the relationship becomes partnership.

The partnership stage of marriage is really about survival, and can be very beautiful. I have watched couples go through difficult trials such as cancer or the loss of a child, and they survive together in a beautifully supportive way.

A Light Theology About Human Conflict

Once the partnership begins to wear down, what is left? Well, for couples who do not know Christ, there is not much left holding them together. As Christians we are committed in marriage because Christ is committed to us! If marriage is a picture of Christ and the church, then marriage is a picture of commitment. In truth, I have certainly seen non-Christian couples committed to their vows just as much as I have seen Christian couples flippantly abandon their vows. When romance, friendship and partnership fade, we are only left with the base blocks of commitment.

Committed marriages are beautiful marriages because they put into daily practice the patient love of Christ. If you are reading this and you are in a commitment level relationship with your spouse, you are representing the commitment of Christ and it is beautiful. It is Gospel rich worship in your daily reality. Keep going!

That being said, the goal of marriage is not just to survive. The goal in marriage is to thrive just as God wants us to thrive in our relationship with Him through the Holy Spirit! The ebb and flow of marriage is the pursuit of rebuilding, constantly rebuilding the layers one block at a time. The goal of marriage should be to find romance in our 70's should God grant us that much life together. To get to romance, I must first build back to partnership. We must not be under the notion that one weekend romantic getaway will fix a broken

Peacemaking - Peacekeeping

marriage relationship. We must start on the level we are on, and over time build back through the levels one level at a time. If you are merely in a committed stage, then work on finding ways to partner together to accomplish some specific goals. Do not be settled with mere partnership. Work towards the friendship level by practicing proper communication skills and working through conflict. If you are stuck at the partnership level, find ways to have fun and create memories as friends. If you are just friends, look for ways to find intimacy afresh that will create a longing to be closer together. Never settle! Flirt and fall in love all over again, every year, with your spouse! The more we learn about our spouse, the more we can fall in love with them! Always push for more of one another; but more importantly, always push to give more to one another. Remember, we learn by asking questions, not by making statements!

Are there marriages that will not be restored? Unfortunately, yes. If you find yourself in that situation, you are called to be a godly peacekeeper. I pray that you will seek the wisdom form the Holy Spirit in how you navigate your situation.

As I close, please remember that God wants the best for every human relationship, not just marriage. God has called us to love him with our heart, soul and mind, and he has called us to love our neighbors with the

A Light Theology About Human Conflict

same intentionality that we love ourselves. Seek the best in every relationship. When possible, make peace! When necessary, keep the peace. In all relationships, learn how you might be more like Christ, thereby possessing peace. **God is working to constantly bring us back into a healthy place in our relationship with him! It is our job to do the same with one another.** I close this book with one more bit of scripture, given to us by the man we have been discussing in this chapter: The Apostle Paul. The following is his final word to the church at Corinth, battling to work through conflict.

> 2 Corinthians 13:11-14
> (ESV)
>
> 11 Finally, brothers, rejoice.
> Aim for restoration, comfort
> one another, agree with one
> another, live in peace; and
> the God of love and peace
> will be with you. 12 Greet one
> another with a holy kiss.
> 13 All the saints greet you.
> 14 The grace of the Lord
> Jesus Christ and the love of
> God and the fellowship of
> the Holy Spirit be with you
> all.

Made in the USA
Middletown, DE
29 October 2023

41474373R00061